P p

pig

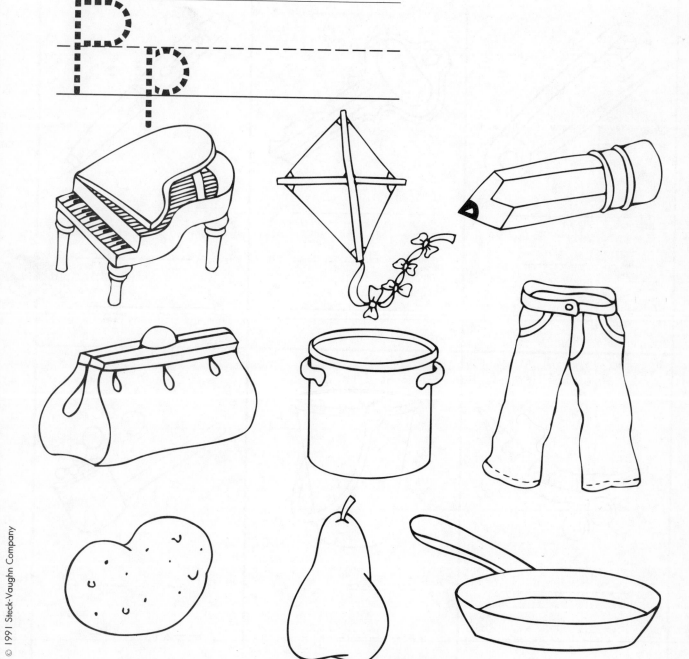

Name _____

Initial p Trace and write the letters. Color the pictures whose names begin with the *p* sound.

1

p p

Initial p Trace and write the letters. Write *p* below each picture whose name begins with the *p* sound.

Nn

nest

Name _____

Initial n Trace and write the letters. Color the pictures whose names begin with the *n* sound.

3

nn

Initial n   Trace and write the letters. Write *n* below each picture whose name begins with the *n* sound.

C c

cat

Name _____

Initial c   Trace and write the letters. Color the pictures whose names begin with the *c* sound.

5

Initial c Trace and write the letters. Write *c* below each picture whose name begins with the *c* sound.

p	p	p
n	n	n
c	c	c

p	p	p
n	n	n
c	c	c

p	p	p
n	n	n
c	c	c

Name _____

Reviewing Initial p, n, c   Circle the letter that stands for the first sound in each picture name.

7

Reviewing Initial p, n, c Color the cart with the *p* red, the *n* yellow, and the *c* green. Then color the items beginning with those same sounds to match.

p

n

p

n

p

n

p

n

p

n

p

n

p

n

p

n

p

n

Name _____

Final p and n Circle the letter that stands for the last sound in each picture name.

9

10   **Final p and n**   Write the letter that stands for the last sound in each picture name.

m	n

 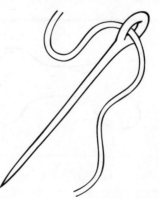 

Name _____

Discriminating Initial m and n Color the box that has the *m* red and the *n* blue. Then color the pictures beginning with those same sounds to match.

11

Discriminating Final m and n Write the letter that stands for the last sound in each picture name.

Hh

hat

Hh

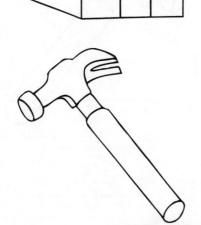

Name _____

Initial h Trace and write the letters. Color the pictures whose names begin with the *h* sound.

h h

Initial h Trace and write the letters. Write *h* below each picture whose name begins with the *h* sound.

L l

leaf

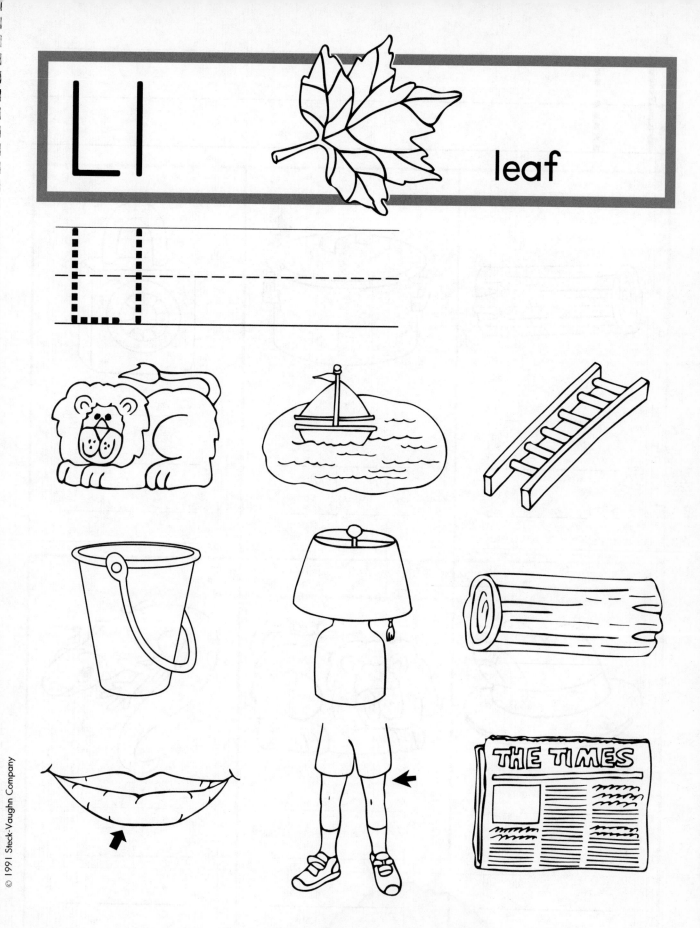

Name _____

Initial l Trace and write the letters. Color the pictures whose names begin with the *l* sound.

15

Initial l Trace and write the letters. Write *l* below each picture whose name begins with the *l* sound.

R r

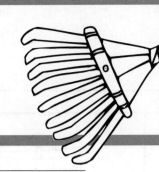 rake

R r

  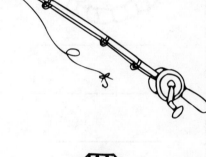

  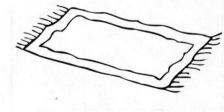

Name _____

Initial r Trace and write the letters. Color the pictures whose names begin with the *r* sound.

17

Initial r Trace and write the letters. Write *r* below each picture whose name begins with the *r* sound.

h l r

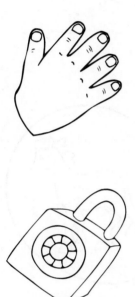

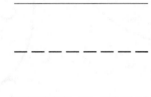

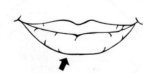

Name _____

Reviewing Initial h, l, r   Write the letter that stands for the first sound in each picture name.

19

20 **Reviewing Initial h, l, r** Color the top balloon that has the *h* blue, the *l* green, and the *r* red. Then color the other balloons that have pictures beginning with those same sounds to match.

Name _____

Final l and r   Circle the letter that stands for the last sound in each picture name.

21

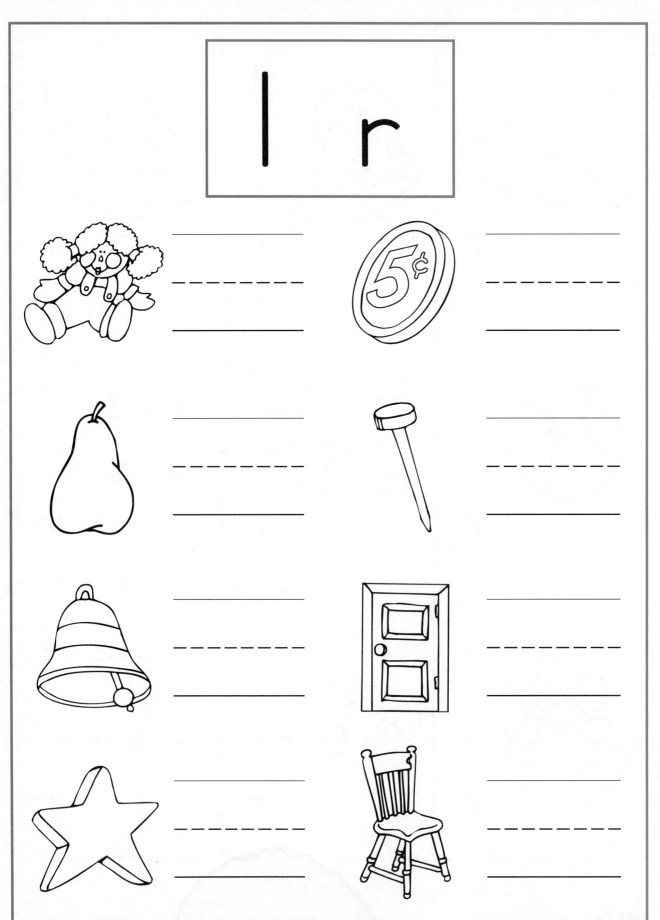

22   **Final l and r**   Write the letter that stands for the last sound in each picture name.

Reviewing Initial **p, n, c, h, l, r** Circle the letter that stands for the first sound in each picture name.

23

Name _____

p n c h l r

Reviewing Initial p, n, c, h, l, r   Write the letter that stands for the first sound in each picture name.

Name _____

Reviewing Final p, n, l, r   Circle the letter that stands for the last sound in each picture name.

25

p n l r

Reviewing Final p, n, l, r   Write the letter that stands for the last sound in each picture name.

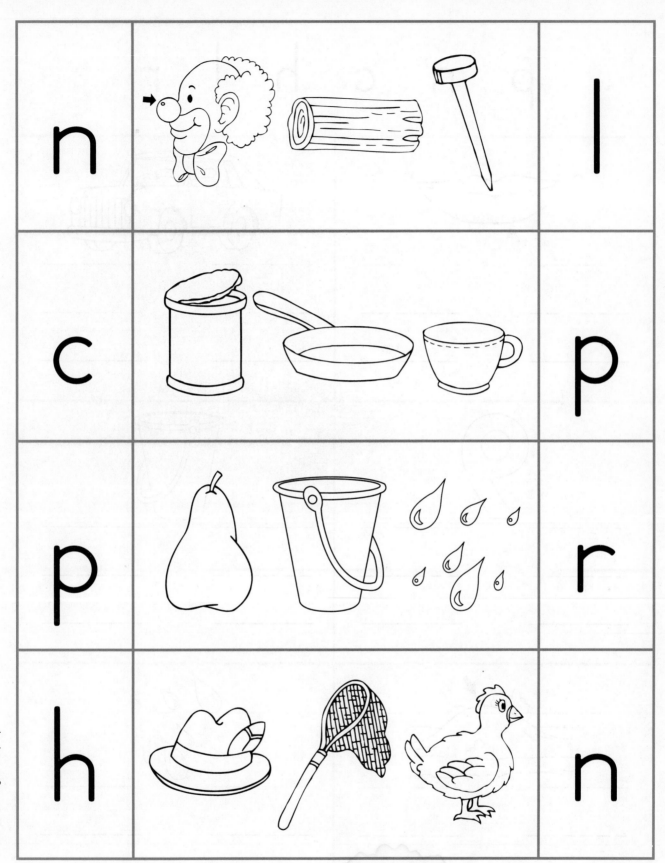

Name _____

Initial and Final p, n, c, h, l, r Color the picture whose name begins with the sound of the letter on the left and ends with the sound of the letter on the right.

27

p n c h l r

Initial and Final p, n, c, h, l, r Write the letters that stand for the first and last sound in each picture name.

V v

vest

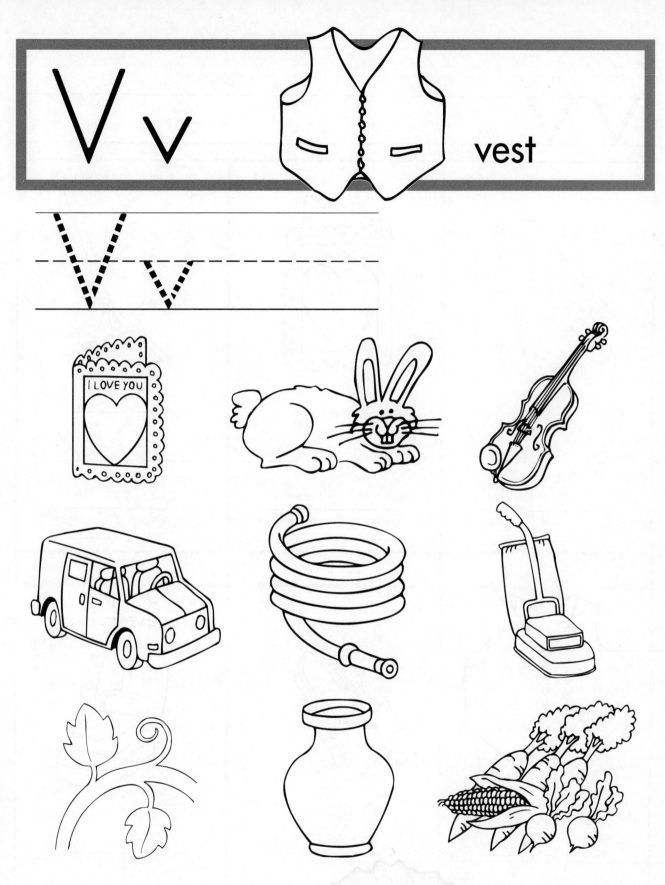

© 1991 Steck-Vaughn Company

Initial v Trace and write the letters. Color the pictures whose names begin with the *v* sound.

V V V

Initial v Trace and write the letters. Write *v* below each picture whose name begins with the *v* sound.

Y y

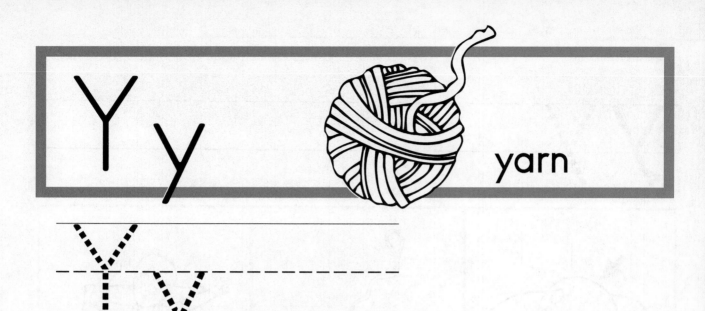

yarn

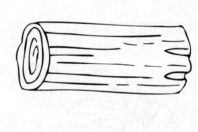

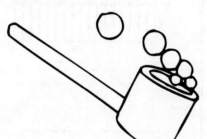

Name _____

Initial y   Trace and write the letters. Color the pictures whose names begin with the *y* sound.

31

Y y

Initial y Trace and write the letters. Write *y* below each picture whose name begins with the *y* sound.

Z z

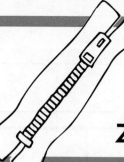

zipper

Z z

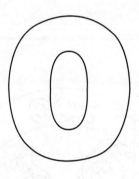  

 ZOO

Name

Initial z   Trace and write the letters. Color the pictures whose names begin with the z sound.

33

Zz

Initial z Trace and write the letters. Write *z* below each picture whose name begins with the *z* sound.

Qu qu

 queen

Qu qu

Name _____

Initial qu Trace and write the letters. Color the pictures whose names begin with the *qu* sound.

ququ

Initial qu Trace and write the letters. Write *qu* below each picture whose name begins with the *qu* sound.

y z qu	v y z	v z qu
v y qu	v z qu	y z qu
v y z	v y qu	y z qu

Name _____

Reviewing Initial v, y, z, qu   Circle the letter or letters that stand for the first sound in each picture name.

Reviewing Initial v, y, z, qu *Color the spool that has the v red, the y blue, the z green, and the qu yellow. Then color the* squares in the quilt that have pictures beginning with those same sounds to match.

X x

ax

Name _____

Final x Trace and write the letters. Color the pictures whose names end with the *x* sound.

39

X x

Final x Trace and write the letters. Write *x* below each picture whose name ends with the *x* sound.

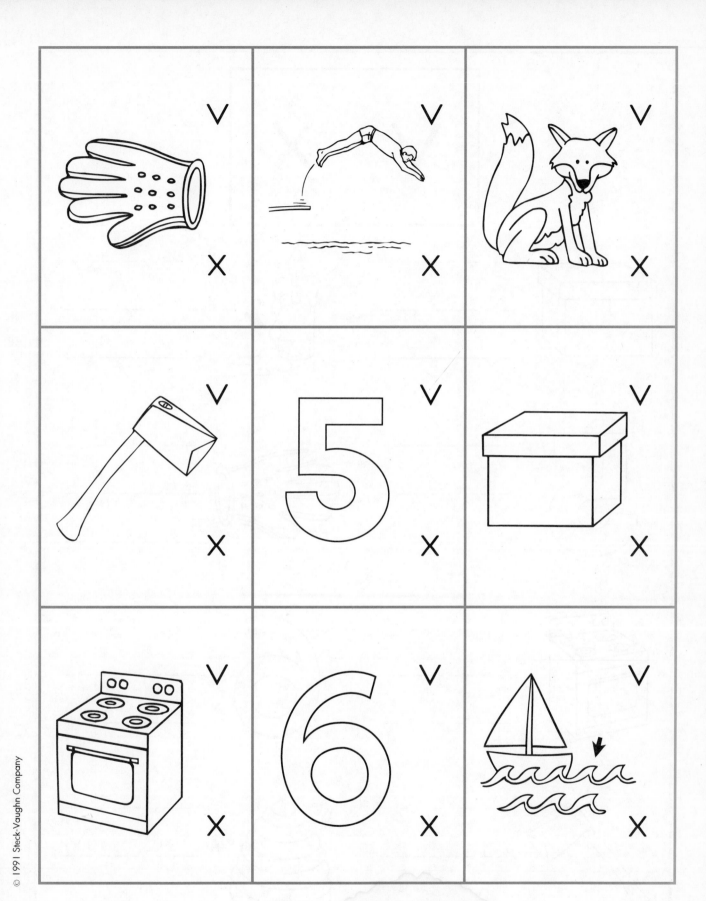

Name _____

Final v and x   Circle the letter that stands for the last sound in each picture name.

41

Final v and x   Write the letter that stands for the last sound in each picture name.

h l r	v y z	p n c
l r z	n c h	qu v y
h y z	p r qu	c qu p

Name _____

Reviewing Initial Sounds   Circle the letter or letters that stand for the first sound in each picture name.

43

p n c h r v z qu

_____

- - - - - - - - - - - -

_____

_____

- - - - - - - - - - - -

_____

_____

- - - - - - - - - - - -

_____

_____

- - - - - - - - - - - -

_____

_____

- - - - - - - - - - - -

_____

_____

- - - - - - - - - - - -

_____

_____

- - - - - - - - - - - -

_____

_____

- - - - - - - - - - - -

_____

44 **Reviewing Initial Sounds**   Write the letter or letters that stand for the first sound in each picture name.

p
n
l

r
v
x

v
x
n

r
l
p

x
l
n

p
r
v

v
x
p

l
r
n

r
p
x

Name _____

Reviewing Final Sounds   Circle the letter that stands for the last sound in each picture name.

45

p n l r v x

_____
_____

- - - - - - - - - -
_____

4
- - - - - - - - - -
_____

- - - - - - - - - -
_____

_____
_____

- - - - - - - - - -
_____

_____
_____

- - - - - - - - - -
_____

Reviewing Final Sounds   Write the letter that stands for the last sound in each picture name.

z		r
r		p
n		l
c		n

Name _____

Reviewing Initial and Final Sounds   Color the picture whose name begins with the sound of the letter on the left and ends with the sound of the letter on the right.

p n c h l r v y qu

_ _ _ _ _   _ _ _ _ _

_____   _____

_ _ _ _ _   _ _ _ _ _

_____   _____

_ _ _ _ _   _ _ _ _ _

_____   _____

_____   _____

_ _ _ _ _   _ _ _ _ _

_____   _____

_____   _____

_ _ _ _ _   _ _ _ _ _

_____   _____

_____   _____

_ _ _ _ _   _ _ _ _ _

_____   _____

Reviewing Initial and Final Sounds   Write the letters that stand for the first and last sound in each picture name.